In the K

Hannah Stephenson

ISBN 10: 0-9859191-2-4

ISBN 13: 978-0-9859191-2-2

Cover image: "Snow as a Girl," Aron Wiesenfeld
(www.aronwiesenfeld.com)
Cover design: Anthea Ben-Naim
(www.behance.net/AntheaKrook)

GOLD Wake Press

Boston, Ma

In the Kettle, the Shriek

For Cindy, and my family

Table of Contents

Town

It starts with a river. Green hills,
and promising flatland beneath them.

All these trees go, and get lugged out
of the clearing. The stone near the water

is brought to the place where the woods
once stood, and also the felled trees that

lived there before, and this is how the town
rises from the ground. Structures answer

the needs of the people there. A church,
a school, a jail, a cemetery. Occupations

grow, more answers. The doctor who
interprets fevers, the midwife, a witness

to how bodies respond to air the first
time they feel it, the man who says

that the town thrives because it was
intended to. Gratitude solves everything.

When plants are plentiful and people live,
the land is grateful to the town for

their goodness. And when it snows for
an extra month, or the little girl drowns

in the river, they are told to look at
pain and then to look past it. To trust

that this land found them, that when
a glacier began melting and dripping

over stone, the river was already
dreaming of the town, calling to it.

From Scratch

Trust the road to hold the car,
the signs to gesture honestly
and without malice. Trust
that a mile on your odometer
means a mile behind you,
a one-mile-sized patch of town
your tires touched and left.
Trust that in the town the dogs
are given food, that their names
are said to them with sweetness,
that fathers in this town hold
their sons' hands when they
are young. Trust that the spiders
stay in their webs high up
in the trees, that the freezer aisle
in the grocery store stays cold
and that the twist ties on the bread
continue to squeeze the plastic
shut around the slices for days
after the *sell by* date, that there
is no guilt in the woman who
pauses before the cake mix
to find the one that requires
the fewest ingredients, eggs
and oil and water, which she has.

Reciprocity

I crush the empty eggshells in my hand
to hold them all.

So it is with cities that we go away from.
That which we leave

swipes slimy fingers over us, slipping out.
What we hang onto

gets compressed, layered. Remembering
destroys the place,

obliterates whatever does not glitter, makes
a new thing for us

to miss. There, the cobblestones long for
the weight of our feet,

and pine needles hold in their fragrance,
no one to appreciate it

properly. But cities are not sad, do not
take note when we move

in or out. So we invent a place, a city that finds
room in it for a memory

of us living within it. Holds us, its crumpled note.
A city of reciprocity.

Telepathy

I want you to think of a deck of cards.
Pick a card. Picture it. Pick only one,
don't make this harder than it is. Black
or red, and what is the suit. You know,
the suit, diamonds, hearts, spades, the other
one. Clover-type thing, a deciduous tree.
Paw print-looking. Imagine the first birthday
cake you ever had. What flavor was the cake.
What shape. What color frosting. Conjure
the taste in your mouth, the scent of smoke
that comes from a small candle blown out
after twenty seconds. Think of your favorite
animal. Any mammal under twenty-five pounds,
really. Any undersized mammal that meows,
hold one in your mind, even if it struggles.
Best to drop it in vertically, I find. Gravity
can be another set of hands. Pick a fjord,
any fjord. Or a volcano. Visualize yourself
standing in front of it, smiling. Wait--smile
again, your eyes were closed in that one.
You're at the volcano, grinning big, I mean
really big, with your eyes totally open
in surprise because someone is standing
next to you with his arm around your shoulders.
Who is it. Who do you see. What does he do
when the ground starts jostling against your feet.
Picture your least comfortable pair of shoes.
Where do they pinch. How do they mark you.
Try these. I've brought the next size up.
Too big now. Choose any planet, except for Earth.
The moon is not a planet. I know, it's weird,
maybe we can swap it in for Pluto, no one's
favorite anyway. Your card, have you forgotten it.
It's here on the floor, your driver's license.
From another state. It's expired. Think of a number
between one and ten, any number. I know it isn't
one or ten. Four, likely. Or seven. Think of me
reaching into your mind as if it were a sink,
full of soapy water. And now, this number is yours.
Whenever I hear it, I will be reminded of you.

The Apartment

People have been living in your home,
the apartment that you rent, for forty years,
fifty years. Who were they. Where did
they go. The apartment remembers them
a little, a kitten sticker on the inside
of the medicine cabinet, a glass turkey
with a divot in its back for a votive candle.
When I moved in to one place, a toaster
tucked in the highest shelf, in the very back.
It was full of crumbs and dust, a record of appetite,
emptiness. A home is our own because
we decide to pour our possessions into
its pockets. It contains us, helps us to know
what we need more of, less of. *Go get wood*
and bring it in here. And matches,
the fireplace says. When we snap back,
And where might we find some wood,
it's not even angry. *Go to the supermarket,*
sweetheart. We obey it. It keeps us apart
from the unpartitioned, cold wilderness.
We want to be who it tells us we are.

Calling

How did you get here.
If you were to tell me,

where would you begin.
What new thing called

to you, installed wheels
under your shoes, gave

you a handlebar and told
you to hold on while it

towed you. What caused
you to drop the anchor

back there, or over here.
When you chose, did you

feel that you were the one
choosing, or was a voice

loudly commanding you.
Did your decision fall

from you, light as a dime
slipping from your wallet,

no sounds, no sensations,
no evidence that the world

requires any thing from us,
any one thing over another.

Signage

Stores die with the same velocity as bugs.
One day, humming, clicking. Shiny doors
parting like beetle wings. And then, gone.
Emptied out. A shell. The sudden voicelessness
of the SupeRx, its sign darkened and waiting
to be pried from the building. The town talks
about it. This is how they mourn. And when
the people of the town encounter those
they know working a till at the grocery store,
or behind bank glass, SupeRx gets stuffed
into the quiet between them. Always *Did you*
hear about the SupeRx, mmhmm, isn't it
a shame. That a strange, new business
can rise to its feet in a body not belonging
to it. Blue signage plastered over yellow.
Shameful, the brutal reincarnation
of buildings. It's a pharmacy again within
the month, sentenced to revisiting sickness,
the earnestness with which we fix ourselves.

Seasonally Affected

The seasons affect us, whether
daylight drains away in the afternoon
or evening. The snow and ice

chase us indoors, slow our steps,
our driving, our blood. We see branches,
bare, as bones. Plants persist

in the winter, but they do not grow.
Evergreen and umber bark instead of pink
or white petals. Shadows bloom

in the tree limbs and thus, some
place inside us. There was once a purpose
for our sadness and fatigue

in winter. We were naked
and cold, or we used to be bears and still
experience the urge to hibernate.

There are many ways to bring
light into your life in the winter. Buy a lamp,
arrange for a mechanical dawn

at your bedside. Tell your cells
that this bulb is the sun transformed into
a potted plant. They may or may not

fall for it. There will always be
darkness in you. What can you build
with it, with your sensitivity.

Of Two Minds

Dear Miss Manners, teach me
how to reach a decision.
When I reach for it, what will
it feel like, fingertips
grazing my fingertips, or just
dead air where we
expect a door knob or wall to be.
Dear Mrs. Mannerisms,
are you the same woman every
place you go, are you Ms.
Matterhorn when you encounter
strangers, are you Miss
Dark Matter in the studio or lab,
Dr. Matter of Fact in
the car, at the bank. Is it polite
to ask someone their
age. Are we obsessed with weight
because our psyches
feel huge, yet we know we were
made to eventually
shed every pound we seem to own,
are we able to look at
our bodies and faces in the mirror
and know how our skin
drapes on the bone. There are spots
we will never see on our
own bodies, my darling Miss Manners.
What is the appropriate
response to that. Did you instruct
pop stars to recreate
epiphany in their songs by way of
key change, gospel choir.
Were you hired as a receptionist
and promoted once they
heard how sympathetic syllables
sounded in your voice,
That one, you, *shows real potential.*

The Twin

She does everything you choose not to
and returns each night while you sleep,
ever loyal. When you are alone, buried
in thoughts like warm sand, then you
feel her there. Whatever you want to give
her, she will take, all of it. Her expertise
is in safe keeping. Her body is made up
of the energy you expend while forming
decisions. She is the sentence unsaid
that afternoon in the car, and the city
you did not visit. She is a runner, fierce,
fearless. Somehow, she learned things
you ignored, how to build molecules,
unscrewing and tightening the atoms,
as if twisting balloons into dogs, rabbits.
Where to clamp which wire when jumping
a dead battery. All the hours sleep has taken
from you have been fed to her. If she could
put her arm around you, she would,
so grateful is she for what you don't do.

We Will Judge You Based on Your Wedding

We will judge you based on your wedding,
on what you have designed. How many guests
were you expecting, and how many are present.
What did you do to the ceremony. How did
you renovate it, what did you rip out and what
did you add. What century does your wedding
take place in. Is it full of *thines* and *beloveds*,
did you invite any God. Who cries. Do you
engender jealousy. What colors did you swath
your bridesmaids in, what necklines. How
symmetrical is your wedding party. Where are
the tall people. Did you pin the flowers
to each groomsman's chest, do the petals
echo the girls' dresses and tablecloths and
place cards. Have you obeyed every tradition
pressed into your hands. Did you give your lipstick
to the maid of honor. Have you asked her
to lift your skirts in the bathroom. When you kiss
your husband, is it tasteful. Do your mouths convey
to your guests how you burn for each other.
Did you tie each little package of bubbles
with ribbon, does each guest breathe across
you when you leave for the reception, a baptism.
Are there butterflies. Or doves. Are they still alive
and able to fly. Who did you seat together.
Is everyone accounted for. Who is here alone,
have you sat them together. Does your photographer
give you enough feedback so your poses look natural.
What memories does the camera create. Will you
smash cake in the face of your partner. Does he know,
will he recoil or laugh and lick his lips. How do
you feel about everyone watching you eat, dance.
They can make you kiss at any time. Will you
grow tired of it. Will you graciously comply.
What song will you select to represent every
emotion coursing through you, will it cause
your guests to run onto the dance floor, cheering.
You are responsible for all of this, your choices
splashed across the reception hall and pouring
out of the speakers. We are submerged in them.
What kind of a woman are you. This is your day.

Little Black Dress

Your must-have, your go-to,
a dark being that loves how
you are put together, how you
are assembled. A woman's
little black dress is essential.
For survival. It lets her get
looked at, assessed. She has
passed. *Now that is what
I call a woman, a real lady*,
someone says, watching
as she walks. The little
black dress is a password,
a code. It is grammatically
correct, anatomically corrective.
The little black dress hides
a multitude of sins. An army
of sins, a swarm of them
surround every woman. She
must be stopped, forgiven.
The fashion police stalk her.
When they catch her they will
spill shame over her head
as sweetly as parents bathing
a little baby. Where is your
little black dress. You must
have one, every woman should.
Go to it, take it in your arms,
pour your body into it. Your little
black dress prepares you for
any occasion, you are more
appropriate wearing it, we can
appreciate its littleness and
its darkness on your body. We
are so relieved you are clothed
in it. How divine you look.

Treehouse for God

All language is shorthand
for a real thing. Listening
for meaning is the act of

interpretation. Which sound
is important, and which
silence. When God says,

Build me a treehouse, you
have to decide: how literal
is this message. *Let me live*

in the branches and trees,
is this what is being said,
or does God want you to

craft ten stories out of wood
from collapsed barns, rooms
and rooms and stairwells

and porches so you can stand
outside of the house while
you are in it. We will see so

little of the world that it is
important for you to see this
tree, to envision rooms and

stairs where there is only air
and leaves, to place the first
board against the bark.

Your Neck of the Woods

How is it going, there
in your neck of the woods.
When you leave your home,
do you step into direct light
or shade. What tree thrives
in your back yard. Do you
look at it through the window
in the morning. Do you
walk into rooms and lose
the task you had set up
for yourself. In the shower,
do you always remember
whether you have washed
your hair yet. Have you
looked for suds in the drain
as a clue. How are you
wearing your hair. In your
neck of the woods,
are the afternoons loud
with lawnmowers and cars.
How quickly does it become
evening for you. Do you
identify with the town
in which you live, where
do you feel you are from.
Who do you speak with
each day, most days, or only
on occasion. Do you share
what you cling to, the ideas
or places or practices, or
is it only visible beneath
your fingernails. Where
is your neck of the woods,
exactly, what portion of
which continent can claim
you. Where are you headed.
There are things about you
I will never know. There are
things I will never know.

Five Second Rule

I drop an almond, pick it up,
examining each side.
I blow on it a little and eat it.
The five second rule
stands, ensures that any fallen
food will remain
uncontaminated if it touches
the floor for no more
than five seconds. Germs need
longer to adequately
contaminate food, crawling
over like an alligator
to claim what you've dropped.
Less than five seconds,
and we can rewind, can undo
time, our fumbling.
Does this apply to laundry,
to warm garments
that we retrieve from the dryer
and let go of, five
seconds until the sock is no
longer clean. Can
the five second rule stretch.
Does it depend on
what is dropped, and where.
How many seconds
would we allot a pillowcase
lounging on the tile
in the laundromat, a lacy pair
of underwear. When
do we need to start over again
with the washer,
a dirty piece of clothing. Could
we use this logic
to reverse any misjudgment
in depth perception,
any mistake or act we drop
into our lives, like
dusting off a parachuter, pulling
him back into the plane
by the crumpled parachute. When

do we even decide
to start counting, is it *one one*
thousand, two one
thousand, or a quick countdown,
New Year's Eve
style, as if time begins whenever
we scream out
the seconds falling from us.

First Things First

Do the first things first,
those things embedded with order
and priority. The urgent things,
the things swirling in your solar plexus
and elbowing you in the heart.

First things first, the things
from which other things spring.
The initial movement, the impulse
to move, the discomfort that triggers
a flicker in your nerves.

First things come first.
You wake, you lift your eyelids,
perform subconscious diagnostics.
What do you need today, you ask
yourself, watching the walls.

First things first, you trust
that by starting the day's processes,
you will go where you need to.
Even the eighth thing you do
can be the first, even the nineteenth thing.

I Could Care Less

I could care less,
I could,
but instead, I care
so much,
so phenomenally.
It happens
when we look, this
mountain
range-sized adoration
welling up
inside us in response
to all that
is present alongside
us, and all
that existed before
the human
thumb squeezed
the top of
the common era's
stopwatch.
The seven holes in our
heads help
us to take in what we
can of the
ever-altering wilderness
here for us,
with us. How is this not
collaboration.

Co-here

We are all of us here
at the same time.
A neighborhood is an
agreement: you
can have your home
near mine. We can
share the grass
between us, and your
floor can be my
ceiling. We can have a
block party, close
roads to cars and eat
picnic food together.
Limit the cooking
to food sliced into
small shapes we know,
cheese cubes, triangles
of watermelon. Our city
should take the day
off, declare a local
holiday. The occasion:
this moment is an
intersection of every life
already in progress,
it just so happens that
we are here in the
presence of one another
and that is what convinces
every collection of
molecules to hold together.

How to Sell a Mattress

A woman jumps on a mattress,
her purple nightie shining under
studio lights. In the corner

opposite her, a wine glass full
of wine, redder than the satin
on her body, but similar, glossy.

She jumps carefully, so the glass
remains level on the white foam,
but she tries not to let her caution

register across her face. *Relax*,
she tells the muscles of her face,
she lifts her brows a bit to signal

surprise, smiles slightly at how
the glass is undisturbed by her
body, her feet sinking into

the forgiving foam of the bed
and lifting from it. The dents
from her feet fill in quickly,

like dough plumping beneath
a damp towel, cooperating
with what we want from it,

for it. A man sits next to her,
looks up at her. In the world
of the commercial, he is her

husband, this is their bed,
they sleep on it without sheets
and they drink wine together

before sleeping every night.
She watches the glass, allows
disbelief to well up in her eyes,

and the husband watches her,
beaming, *Honey, I am so proud
of you.* With this new bed,

she will never wake him when
she gets up because she cannot
sleep, and when she finally does

close her eyes, she will not
feel him shifting around in his
sleep as he usually does, the dreams

twisting him, rotisserie-style.
This mattress is a gift. They will not
know the other one is even there.

Suddenly, Pasta Salad

Suddenly, pasta salad.
All of a sudden,
pasta salad appears.

Voila! Spontaneous
occurrence of noodles
and diced vegetables,

rotini sprouting up
at your feet like tulips
in a time-lapse video.

No time in this realm
in which pasta salad
instantly materializes,

a perfect being, offering
itself to you without
needing your touch

or your knife. Vacant
space solved through
cold carbohydrates, as if

cooked and then bowled
and cellophaned and
refrigerated, lovingly.

Selfless and sudden,
pasta salad. It wants
to be eaten, it tastes

like a miracle, whipped
up in a kitchen both
invisible and close by.

The opposite of nothing
is pasta salad, whole
entities become ingredients

and the completeness
of pasta conceals the flour
in its DNA, the wheat.

Creation looks like this,
one minute nothing,
and then, pasta salad

as if thrown down
from above, pasta ex
machina, a solution.

It has come for you
because you wanted it
and if you didn't

you do now. The longer
you look at it
the more real it is,

the more you can envision
eating it, selecting
a possible chef to thank.

Your Name on a Grain of Rice

Your name on a grain of rice.
Your name, tiny, encapsulated.

Your name scribbled on a white
grain of rice, kept in an amulet.

Your name strung around your
own neck on a black satin cord.

Your name burned into matter.
Your name, a touchable thing.

Your name spoken to a stranger
whose hands grapple with it.

Your name, a way to remember
yourself walking on the beach.

Your name, of the rice itself.
Your name, organic, growing.

Your name rising from within
the rice to meet the outer world.

Your name, given to you, which
you give to or etch in others.

Psalm Dot Com

Read aloud, URL's sound much
like prayers, *http* unpronounceable
as the name of a god, the voice
leaving after dot com, amen,
awmain. Who is listening to
our searching. We are, and so is
everyone. Knowledge sprouts
communally, spreads across
oceans in instants. Hive mind
dot com. Ring of mushrooms
dot org. We talk to people
through our fingers, a typed out
stage whisper aimed at one
listener or all. The @ sign
is conversational, shows how
words can be loosed deliberately,
shows our hand steadying the arrow
of speech. We cannot touch
meaning, but we can gesture
toward it, point at it, point it out
for others in the room so they
can share with their grandchildren
what it was like, beauty dot edu,
a great calm dot com. #Amen.

Lorem Ipsum

To see design more clearly, sprinkle tormented
gibberish across the page, flouring a countertop

so dough can be flattened on it. *Lorem ipsum
dolor sit amet, consectetur, adipisci velit.*

The letters are a page. To a reader, they signify
Your name here, a story about the work you do,

about all you have accomplished and built.
In these pretty words, breath and boundary.

*Lorem ipsum dolor sit amet. Blah blah
blah reverberating.* It is sweet and becoming

to erect paragraphs, cardboard cut-outs standing
in for architecture. Don't lean on that column,

or look too closely at this text. It is only here
to protect us from silence, to invoke the pretense

of grace, greeked. What can fill this lonely room.
Lorem ipsum dolor sit amet, consectetur, adipisci velit,

nonsense, scissored Cicero loosely translated as
There is no one who loves pain itself, who seeks

after it and wants to have it, simply because it is pain.
Embroider it on dust ruffles, print it on potpourri.

Spell it out in refrigerator magnets, exposed beams,
this, a most versatile text. Use its invocation

to decorate. Design something for your reader,
and in the meantime, let them see your intentions.

Murmur it into their cheek, the spine of a book,
a page: *lorem ipsum,* I am working on it now.

You Can Do This

You have parallel parked in a space
just five inches bigger than your car,
smoothly. You know Queen Anne's lace
from poison hemlock. You are
adept in remembering names,
and people's small quirks, you know
who has cats or dogs, who trains
them. You know an Aries from a Virgo,
a Libra from a Taurus. You have worked
at 4 AM, or for 15 hours in one shift,
spoken cheerfully while your life jerked
and jolted. You found a gown in a thrift
shop, and it is beautiful. You are learning
to call to what you love, to see it returning.

You Are Here to Receive This Prophecy

You are here to receive this prophecy,
I am so certain of this I would wager life on it.

Get open, fast. Get to the highest point
available, that hill, for example. Even better,

the tree on top of the hill. Clamber up,
go on. Do what the branches do, reach up,

tilt your face to the clouds. Now you wait.
Prepare to hear. You never know what the voice

will sound like, perhaps not a voice. Maybe
like a current of electricity sizzling, sparking,

or the snap of knuckles cracking. A slide whistle
or kazoo--don't laugh, it could happen.

How would that look, God talking to you,
you laughing it up in a tree on a hilltop.

Be a lightning rod, an antenna. Reception
can be active, you know. Think of a dancer

being lifted, all her muscles tightening
around her bones. She is lighter for how she

lifts herself, gets smaller, more powerful.
Call the message to you, show you can

be trusted to hear and hold it. Don't even think
of coming down from there, you just wait.

You stay up in that tree, listening. The words
will come to you, they will, they will.

Serious Stuff

The speed limit on this country road
reads *85.* Looks like
someone's been talking back to signs
with black spray paint.
DO NOT cock BLOCK DRIVE, one sign
admonishes without
dropping character. This is serious stuff,
they insist sternly,
all caps lock and black and yellow.
They don't realize
what they've said, their Freudian slips.
How little modification
these signs require to be turned inside out:
the three folds back
on itself like a turned page to become an eight,
four letters squirm
their way between the lines of text. Someone
walked to the side
of the road last night, eying the signs plopped
atop their metal posts.
Before his brain told his hand to grab the can
of paint, it processed
this thought: *What else could these signs
tell us to do.*
What can I make using these rules.

In the Kettle, the Shriek

In the kettle, the shriek.
In smooth gums, the teeth.

In a heart, the hole.
In the flat page, the fold.

In the skin, the scar.
In quartz or flint or granite, the spark.

In juniper, the gin.
In the shut window, the wind.

Photographs of Flowers

In the morning, the red tulips
are closed, but when I return
at night, their petals are open
and looking for light, black centers
exposed, pinprick pupils.
I want to photograph them
and the flowering trees along
the street, the pear blossoms
and the magnolias. The petals
are already tearing off
and being blown into the road.

The park is full of people
holding cameras out in front
of them like maps. How close
can they zoom in on a petal,
a bee, a stamen. This is almost
like pornography, the flower
lying there, open before
our eyes, the camera we crouch
with. The flower's stillness,
and our scrutiny, our breathing.
Those we love, we pose them
in front of flowers, petals next
to their faces. This is how we
talk to them about their beauty.

In Silos

In winter, salt. In spring, mud.
The changeover offers up the ground.
Every year, I am startled at its softness.

At white buds in the trees.
Cardinal swooping across the road
and into the bushes, a snapped red ribbon.

Black cows on a green hill,
gathered in circles and facing one another.
The problem is we're operating in silos.

I write in the speech bubble
over their heads what I've heard so often
at meetings. As if we were each silver pillars,

little bits of grain rattling
along the walls within us. We are,
but we are also stocked with the ability

to feel astonished at how
blossoms and leaves are tucked
into the sleeves of dark branches, at how

the season will help us begin
a garden or change the purpose of a room.
This spring is nothing or just like last year's.

Dorothy Gale, Where Are Your Parents

Dorothy Gale, where are your parents.
Did they die. Did you ever know them,
did you come to accept their absence
gradually. Uncle Henry and Aunt Em,
are you related to them by blood.
How old were you when you first
came to the farm. Were you good
to them. Polite, all ma'ams and sirs,
or gushy and affectionate, Uncle Hen,
Auntie. How did you find Toto.
Were you born in Kansas. When
the sky goes sepia before a tornado,
how do you react to the wind's wail
while it yanks at the door like a hangnail.

Alarm

Alarm sounds like: whoop whoop.
Find your exit. Take the stairs.
Remain calm. Most likely, it's a drill.

Alarm sounds like: rasping shriek,
a hawk. Get under a desk.
This is your test. How quickly can

you hide, can you leave. Do you take
the hand of someone slower.
What or who do you leave behind.

Alarm sounds like: periodic beep.
Be alert. Step into the hallway.
Wait for instruction. From someone.

Alarm sounds like: a swarm of bees.
Because the bees are here. Close
your mouth and eyes, do not flap

your limbs. This is happening, the noise,
the bees. You are not on fire.
You may be stung, but you will live.

Pleasing

Let me be more of what you want.
I mean,
let me be more of what you want,
please.
I want to fix the wound you did
not know
you had until you met me, and felt
memories
being stitched to new purposes,
all of this
should have happened the way that
it did.
Let me accompany you as you wake
and drive
and walk to the grocery store, let us
both be
reminded of crayons when we see
the glossy
produce, the Granny Smith apples and
yellow,
orange, and red bell peppers. We can
wince
together when every black bird in Ohio
shoots
across the sky, planets in fast forward,
skipping
town. I can help you remember which
tiles
and steps are slick when they are wet,
or your
shoes are. When you slip and fall, and
earn
a bruise or scratch, hold it out so I
can praise
it before it fades into a scar, and then,
hold it
out for me to see again, your body healing
itself.

Comfy

We yearn to feel comfortable,
to imagine that the world babies us.

We baby the word, swaddle it
in down blankets, coo *comfy* into

the fleeced sheets. Discomfort
is temporary, we learn as infants,

as children, but even as adults
we pretend that comfort, fullness,

warmth will never lapse. *Why
is this happening*, we cry out

when it does, as the tabletop
inches out from under our hands,

place settings rattling in front
of us, knives and spoons clanking,

and then it is ripped away
from us, the floorboards, too, flaking

and splintering as they fall
into the windy, cavernous darkness.

Just as we locate our center
of gravity, the chaos fairy visits at night,

loops lead weights around
our limbs, ties balloons to our hearts.

In the morning, we wrap
ourselves in blankets, close our eyes.

Just five more minutes,
we implore our consciousness.

The Outside In

This autumn, bring the outside in
to your home. Snip a small branch

from the tree you admire most,
the Japanese maple, or the neighbor's

corn-colored honey locust, and
fasten the leaves to your front door.

Upholstery tacks will work, or
push pins. Even duct tape can look

attractive if you cut it in a fall-like
shape. Trace an oak leaf onto the tape

with a ballpoint pen, and, using
scissors or a crafting knife, carefully

slice the silver tape into the shape
you've drawn onto it. Electrical tape

can also be festive, and is available
in a variety of autumnal hues. Use

the leftover cardboard spools as bark.
Flatten them, hack them apart, and

sprinkle them into a rusty bucket
with some pinecones and red M&M's.

Place your faux-pourri on top of
the TV, on a windowsill, or hang it

over your bed. Get inspired by decay.
When you rake the leaves, allow them

to decompose for a week or so, to sit
in the rain. Reach into the bottom

of the pile, and pull out the slimiest
foliage you can find. Ball it up

in cellophane. Repeat, at least ten
times, and hang the dead leaf bundles

on fishing line. Drape your fall garland
around doorways or appliances. Don't

make this harder than it is. Think *entropy*.
Think of the sugar-clogged veins of leaves,

how they redden in the cold and sun.
When it rains, open the windows of your home

to the water. Soggy wallpaper says fall.
Douse the kitchen tile in applesauce.

Powder the woodwork with nutmeg.
Find the darkest lipstick you can, and

let out the fermented thoughts you've
been saving up, scribble on the mirrors

and walls. Keep your message seasonal,
let it fall apart in your hands. See how easy

it is to create a cornucopia of deterioration,
to inject your home with autumn. Show me.

My Cards

Let me show you my cards.
Which one should I choose.
Which is best. Am I allowed
to play any of these, or are
my options limited. Every
time I play this game I need
to relearn it. Does it annoy you
to explain it to me, what does
it mean that I still can't play
it on my own. A solo is
a duet, my fingertips on
the cold keys, your invisible
hands over mine, pushing,
lifting. Show me your chords,
and I will help you play them
with more feeling, make them
more Italian and deliberate.
My turn to play ghost, to turn
pages and clamp your foot
to the damper pedal. Does
knowledge become a part
of us, do our cells slurp
it up and store it, as bread
absorbs and retains the flavor
of the bananas it is kept next to.
Learning, another digestive
process our bodies excel in,
and just as fickle. Why these
thoughts, scrawled onto the
cave wall of the mind, melody,
nursery rhymes, phone numbers,
but not others, recipes, verb
conjugations in French, the way
to lay out a chess board, and
how the pieces move and attack.

What Panic Wants

Panic wants the full attention of your senses,
twists your dials so that the frequencies collide
and cancel one another out.

The creak in your doorway in the late night
prevents you from seeing anything, even
as you clench the comforter

and search the room for figures or changes
in how the familiar shadows are positioned.
As if to pull an insect

from your eyelashes, panic holds you
by the shoulder, stares at you in concentration,
Stay right where you are.

Your panic wants to protect you, to wrap
thin, cold arms around you and bring you close
to its trembling body.

Your immobility, panic wants this, to stall
all decisions. Panic wants you to look down
and be frightened of how far

you are from the ground, how much farther
you will have to go. It wants you to cling
to the side of this building,

clutching at you as you hold it in your arms.
Stay here with me like this a while longer,
it begs, *we are not ready.*

Sanity Prayer

The things that are going to happen,
let me let them.

What plummets toward me due to gravity,
let it come.

What seeks me out like a homing pigeon,
find me here.

That which I holler and holler for, let it
listen to me.

That which sparks with no warning, I will
not expect it.

Alongside me in the dark, opportunities
accompany me.

Alongside me, my shadow, which moves
when I do.

Around me, havoc I ask for and havoc
unsolicited.

Around me is a forcefield made from
observation.

Let things happen to me, these things or others,
I will participate.

We Were Engineered to Want

We were engineered to want,
to search for whatever can occupy
our hollows. Every type of hunger
is biological. Our bodies are babies,
brats. It is a basic human need
to have needs. Can you picture
a civilization already fully satisfied,
no reaching. We want for ourselves
and for others. The people we love,
when we study them as individuals,
can seem frail, unaccompanied.
We drape our needs over them
to solve their empty-handedness.

Going Through

Through, and into
what. Mink and fox
coats, hinterland.

If it's too dark
to see, your hands
will become your eyes,

reaching into the air
ahead of you, reporting
back to your brain

what is coming. Who
is in the wardrobe
with you, maybe

a dog, a guide,
a witch, or a ghost,
clothed in the sheets

that used to stretch
across your childhood
bed, white with

pale blue blossoms,
blinking at you
through the eyelets.

You are going through
this so you can learn
where it leads,

where you are leading
yourself. You are.
You make your way,

we say, just as we
stage our dreams,
enact and watch them.

Great Migration

Patterns on china have begun
to show evidence of a great migration.
Waves roll out to a plate's edges,
drop off, are absorbed into carpet.
In the stock-still water, feeling no wind,
cranes panic and launch, beat their wings
with such force that nearby villagers
mistake them for dragons.
Smaller birds leave their nests in the trees,
head for the dark, unporcelain woods.
Lovers no longer come here
to sit on the grass together,
discovering speechless ways to speak.
They stay away from this place.
The land here isn't fed by any source.
Parents shield their children's eyes,
pull them close when passing the pond.
Someone should do something, they mutter
and leave the land to its calm disintegration.

They Flee

Ok, you're beautiful, the snow is caught
around your eyes as it falls. So what.
Your limbs are long and slim, poplar,
birch. I pledge to say what you are,
to try, to see you within all beings
that I watch. The three deer, fleeing
the hill after staring at me through
my windshield. Their loping ascent into
the woods, away from the road. But
how do they become the beloved. What
do they have to do with you. The land
willingly transforms for me, will stand
still so I can look, brings me snow,
deer, dawn. I look, even as they go.

In Sink

In sink with one another.
In black hole. A vortext,

a message spun of shards
and the air to carry them.

A doppler radar map
bouquet, red in the center,

green at the edges, Venus
fly trap's clamp and gulp.

In vertigo. In mudslide.
In bear hug of the blender.

In nuclear fusion with
each other, in supernova.

How did you meteorite.
Was it lava at first sight.

Ghost Stories

Because fire coaxes the carbon from wood
and releases it back to the atmosphere,
we gather around it and watch.

It is our favorite kind of destruction, contained,
intentional. We made it, and it makes
itself, burns whatever we feed it.

Fireside talk turns to ghosts. It is inevitable.
A spirit speaking through the stereo,
sparking light bulbs, blown fuses.

A familiar presence but no body, hovering.
The scent of this person we loved,
it overwhelms us and evaporates.

Above, the trees press against the dark sky,
the world's shattered windshield.
Smoke lifts toward it, a ghost.

The Unspoken

What percentage of true things
goes unspoken, held within
a head like the yolk in an egg.
How much of the unspoken
is present as you live, strung
in the rafters and corners,
quiet as cobwebs or blazingly
hot as stage lights. How much
of the unspoken has asked you
to say it. Has demanded to be
uncaged. Has the unspoken
ever spun in your mouth,
shoving itself into the backs
of your teeth, and how difficult
was it for you to sweep it back
and swallow it. Were you stern
or patient with it. As long as you
are able to think, unspoken truths
will wait for you to change them,
to let them out and let them go.

Personal Space

In the airport, we fill every
other seat, leave one empty

out of respect for each other's
personal space, which means

that the energy coming off
our bodies needs somewhere

to go. In public, we leave
room for other people's auras,

acknowledge the haloes
and shadows pinned to us.

Our minds are generous
in deciding human outlines,

knowing we require extra air
and distance, the *there* in *Hi there.*

When someone who used to be
there is gone, the space cleared

is bigger than they were, as
so much snow is displaced

by the maker of a snow angel
once they get up from the ground.

First Cavity

Years without visiting the dentist, and still
I hoped for flawless teeth, the doctor's gloved
digit squeaking against the sleek enamel.
I fantasized about the voices above

my wide-open mouth: *My word, these teeth and gums
are perfect, naturally perfect. You must floss
every day.* From the x-ray tech, a thumbs
up and a grin, *Y'know, it's all because*

she [me] *was born with an advantage--
good material, little need
for maintenance.* But there it was. At the edge
of my next to last tooth on the bottom, a cavity.

It was bound to happen, I consoled myself.
Holes catch up with us, grab on, bind
their destructive bodies to ours. Decay dwells
on us, in us, all around. *Mine,*

a possessive pronoun, a self claimed, owned.
But also a bored-out mountain, a tunnel into stone.

Pressing Ghosts

One morning, my mind woke up
but my body did not go anywhere.
I summoned my extremities, but
they remained slack against
the mattress. It soon wore off,
like drunkenness. Sleep paralysis,
science explains. Muscle lagging
behind consciousness a bit
more than usual. In folklore's
jurisdiction, this is known as
a pressing ghost, *kanashibari.*
The condition of being fastened
with unseen metal, of being held
down by shadow. *Don't get up,*
the pressing ghost murmurs above us,
and we don't. Eventually, they release
us, wheel away into the air like bats.
Your hesitation before unlatching
your guitar, the way you cringe before
bringing your fingers to its strings
if anyone else is with you. Each fear
dripping within you, as water droplets
form at the end of icicles and fall.
This, too, is a pressing ghost. *You will
look stupid,* one says. Or *You can
never finish this.* I'll show you mine:
They will think you are selfish.
The things you make are unremarkable.
How to deal with the spirits of paralysis.
Let us form a strategy. When doubt
presses itself across my chest,
issuing its fine mist of deprecation,
selfishhhh, dullnessss, I will not move
because I cannot, but I will look at it
and answer with this thought:
Even so, I keep creating, I am capable.
I will calmly allow its heaviness
and stand when it goes. It will.

Drownding

Drownding, some say,
as if you are drowned
and it will not stop,
the water keeps
drownding you.

How strangely accurate
this is of endings
and the pain we feel
in participating
in them.

Ending, that *-ing*
an ember, the smoke,
the smell of smoke
so long on your coat
and in your hair.

Not closure. A door
endlessly closing
and approaching
the doorway.
Closed enough.

We stand in decisions
like waders, knowing
we cannot finish
every thing we have
taken and started.

Fatal Flaw

Water is the enemy of technology.
Think of the appliances you have drowned:

a watch dropped in a full bathtub,
a laptop submerged by a toppled glass,

a camera taken by the ocean
as you tried to photograph the color of water,

blue in its entirety, but transparent
and colorless where it casts itself over the sand.

Water can outsmart us with indifference.
It travels everywhere, resides in all creatures,

is rain, and snow, and mist, and ice,
and pond, and lake, and puddle, and cloud.

Water is intelligent, responsive.
It will move when nudged, will spill into

whatever it lands on, finds any hole
or crack and falls into it. Just as every superhero

has a fatal flaw, technology is undone
when it gets wet. Water is the arch-nemesis,

but also the long-haired love interest,
the aunt and uncle and mentor and butler.

What we need, what fuels our strength--
our vulnerability flows from and originates here.

Living Among Us

The former tenants of this planet
left behind housewarming gifts:
blueprints for birds and alligators.

Dinosaurs should get credit for more
creatures, house cats, stick bugs,
the Loch Ness monster, armadillos.

If every living thing is the result
of what existed and perished before it,
how can we not see dinosaurs

living among us, leashed and barking
in front yards, building nests in vowels
of grocery store signs, driving hybrids

on the freeway. *All of us can go away*,
that is the truth lurking in the bones
we hang and frame on museum walls.

We make the dinosaurs names now,
but how were they known to each other.
When it all ended, what did they feel,

what did they see. How high is the pain
threshold of a dinosaur. Did they know
that theirs was an extraordinary ending,

communal, or did they each slip from
consciousness, privately processing
the individual calamity of being stopped.

Did they look up at the asteroid hurtling
toward them, or watch as debris blocked
out all light around them. Did they stare,

like those baby alpacas I pass every day,
standing in grass, craning their necks
so that they can gaze up into the rain.

After After

After after, there is
always more, another
after and another
sewn together, leaving
like the train trailing
behind the bride's
wedding gown and
dragging across carpet,
then tile, pavement,
and grass and eventually,
car upholstery.
Childhood trains us
to expect the great ocean
of time around us,
endless, and always more
of it rolling in and away.
A couple of decades
in, and we know scarcity,
know that birthdays
grow stronger and faster,
are tireless sprinters
who find us and lap us.
There will always be
another and a next
and an after, even if we
are unable know about it.

Afterlife

These are the facts: when you die,
you become the internet.
Nothing is lost. Just a trade in energy
being made, cells for pixels,
memories for information. You will
carry images. You, the glue
between email and attachment. You,
the solvent that eats words
typed into search engines, and you,
the predictive echo, suggesting
what the typist might be seeking out.
The internet is the room
where the afterlife happens. Death
is the hallway. The afterlife
is communal consciousness. All answers
are available and shared.
When typists gaze into their computers,
clicking on links, and time
falls away like a dropped, damp towel,
their fingertips have brushed
the generosity and space awaiting them.

Saying Grace

Dear Dinosaurs, we thank you
for not eating us
not because you couldn't have,
but because we
were never roomies. Thank you
for growing here,
for thriving in colonies and
letting your feet
press down into the ground.
How did you sleep,
were you nervous about your
babies knowing
which plants were poisonous
and which mountains
oozed lava. What were your
dreams like, simply
an extension of your day,
eating, swimming,
stepping over water onto grass
or sand. Or did you
dream past your capabilities,
T. Rex twitching
her little arms, imagining flight.
Did you envy
other dinosaurs, their height
or claws or teeth.
We thank you for dying and
for letting your
bodies fall, for blessing our travel
and machinery
by letting the earth digest you
and allowing us
to witness your canonization,
bones into gasoline.

Long Time No See

When was it that
we last saw one
another.

We use our whole
conversation to
uncover when,

picking through
events and dates,
eliminating

the times we did
not meet by
mentioning

and discarding
them, pulling
the peanut

shells with no
peanut inside
from the bag.

It is satisfying
to sort the years
by talking

to each other,
each comparing
our skulled-up

versions of how
we've forked
over time.

We Look for Migration

For months now,
I notice what seem

to be leaves floating
and flapping in the air

over the freeway, above
my windshield and car.

Butterflies. Buttery
yellow and orange,

mottled brown.
I see them and drive

beneath them,
their small, fervent

thrashing. Winged
things always look

like they are leaving.
Above the butterflies,

clusters of black birds.
For months, I've read

the scattered tea leaves
of their flight as departure.

Where we look for
migration, we will see

migration. If we anticipate
what we think we know

is coming, we won't be
as startled by what it

brings, the evening where
the afternoon once was.

Enchanted/Haunted

When the fridge unplugs itself,
coughing up a couple of cubes
of ice onto the floor,
and reaches its cord out like a tentacle
and slowly scoots away
from the wall.

When the piano whinnies
and snorts through its keys.

When one fork squeezes
its tines from the drawer,
scans the room, and signals
to the others that they
can begin their expedition.

When the lightbulbs unscrew
themselves, and spin as they fall
toward the floor so they won't
break when they drop.

When the electrical outlets
erupt in a chorus of ooohs.

When the kitchen faucet confesses
to the carpet what it would like
to do to it.

At night, when your objects
come to life and scurry
around your home
as you know they do,
what kind of castle
do you feel you live in.

Curb Your God

Gravitate to the shore, to the edges
of land. Go to the water, go in it,
fall off the globe. California ends,
disintegrates: loose soil, sand, saltwater.
This is where we play, at the fringe,
in the rubble. Our country, the bear rug.
We crawl toward its claws, feel for
the floor in the darkness beneath it.
No dogs, the sign says, but here
in the waves, a black dog. He bucks
toward dry sand, notched branch in
his jaws. Mouth antlers. A ruler
between his teeth. *Look what I found
for you*, he would shout out if he could,
and lunges toward his human carrying
a devotion so huge that the world tilts.

Structurally Sound

How softly should beginnings begin
so they mark a shift in sound, yet
do not startle you away, listener.
First silence, then the first stirrings
of intended noise. Fingers lifting to
strings, oxygen sucked into a mouth,
numbers. *One two three, two two three,*
the song is here. We can step into it,
inhabit it, its voice feels familiar.
The chords, the walls. The melody,
the light, and harmonies for windows.
We want to live inside of it, to bask
in sound waves. If we can stay here,
we will never die, will never not know
that plain objects possess magic
that we activate, the silver stapler,
the glossy calendar, the brick building
against the gray sky, these can shimmer
with longing when we look at them
with the right eyes. Generosity, yours,
calls out, and every sound comes
inching out to greet you, the tambourine
and the hands that hold and collide
with it, the obedient guitar strings.
The chorus, a succession of beds
for you to choose from and climb
into. You know this will end, that
minutes will paddle faster and faster,
the song will retreat as you chase it,
transpose itself into a higher key,
beatific. The gospel choir, an aerial
view of what you will soon return to
as it approaches. *See how natural*
endings are, the outro croons,
as a whole house scuttles away,
dragging the block behind it
like a billowing, sparkling nebula.

Fraction

One day, my heart will stop beating. (not everything is a joke)
-Jimmy Kimmel, in a tweet (@jimmykimmel), January 13, 2012

There will be a world with no you in it,
and it won't be lopsided here without you.
The people who knew you will also be
gone, and then the people who had been
told about you. A child in each playground
swing, a dog at the end of every leash.
Water will course through the pipes
in the city you no longer live in, in your
home that you are not inside of. The new
inhabitants will hold a pot beneath
the faucet in the kitchen, place the pot
on top of the stove, just as you did.
Some of your objects remain, have
been reassigned. Your guitar is held
by a boy whose mother purchased it
from a resale shop. Your gray pearls
are with a woman flecked with your
genes. Many of your books have
disintegrated. A few of the things
you made still belong to someone
else who looks at them. There are
television shows starring humans who
were born long after you disappeared.
Feathers fill the pillows, and teens
and preteens take the risk of placing
their tongues in each other's mouths.
Forever, you will never come back.
Ninety-eight or eighty-three over
infinity, it is almost not even a fraction.

Bang

One future: we will keep expanding,
the universe stretching, loosening.

A puddle growing, reaching tidal digits
into antimatter. Muscular arms dragging

the universe outward, claiming space
unspoken for. No box to hold this

galloping creature, no fence to halt
the monster, purposeful, uncoiling.

The other future: we will retreat, slowly
at first. A galaxy hemmed, inching

its skirts back in. Then swifter, stronger
as it recognizes old pieces of itself

falling away. A boomerang, a tethered
hawk. Stars condensing, clanging against

the sinking ground. The universe banging
its toys together, rushing to clear the floor.

Acknowledgments

To the editors and staff of the following publications (where some of these poems previously appeared), a hearty thank you! I am grateful and proud that:

"Town" appeared in Room Magazine.
"From Scratch," "Lorem Ipsum," "Ghost Stories," "We Look for Migration," "After After," "Long Time No See," and "Fraction" appeared in the Huffington Post.
"How to Sell a Mattress" appeared in Heavy Feather Review.
"Your Name on a Grain of Rice" appeared in Escape Into Life.
"You Are Here to Receive This Prophecy" appeared in Qarrtsiluni.
"They Flee" appeared in Tweetspeak poems.
"The Twin" appeared in Contrary.
"Living Among Us" appeared in The Curator.
"Curb Your God" appeared in Fiddleblack.

Many thanks to those who helped this book take shape: J. Michael Wahlgren, Editor Extraordinaire; Anthea Ben-Naim, beautiful designer and inspiring presence; and Aron Wiesenfeld, an artist who I've always admired.

This book could not exist without the love and wisdom of my teachers, creative community, friends, and family. Thank you, David Baker and Amy Gerstler, for your support! Thanks to Ellen, Avery, Geraldine, Cortney, Sara, Leslie, and all of my friends who provide encouragement and countless coffee/cupcake dates. Thank you to those who read The Storialist, and to those who attend Paging Columbus. Thanks to my sister, Mara, who teaches me to dance stupider and embrace silliness; to my mom, Anne, who is unafraid to learn and grow, and to shower those she loves with love (and baked goods); and to my dad, Jack, who helped me love words and the world's webbyness. Thank you to Chuck and David, Susan, Brandon, Brooke and Justin, and the rest of my extended family.

Thank you to Cindy Stephenson--as soon as you knew I was a writer, you'd ask me when my book was coming out. Thank you for your openness and warmth--you are always in my thoughts.

Most of all, thank you to Marcus Stephenson, the best partner I could ask for. You have endlessly cheered me on, encouraged me to take important risks, and talked me off of every ledge. Thank you, and I love you!

Hannah Stephenson is a poet, editor, and instructor living in Columbus, Ohio. She is a poetry blogger for The Huffington Post, and her poems have appeared in publications that include Hobart, Room, Contrary, MAYDAY, qarrtsiluni, and The Nervous Breakdown. In 2013, she served as Editor for *The Ides of March: An Anthology of of Ohio Poets* (Columbus Creative Cooperative). She is the founder of Paging Columbus!, a literary arts monthly event series. You can visit her daily poetry site, The Storialist, at www.thestorialist.com, or drop her a line at hannahjstephenson@gmail.com.

CPSIA information can be obtained at www.ICGtesting.com
Printed in the USA
BVOW03s0203240713

326610BV00001B/8/P